Let's Learn About Story Elements: Character

Let's Learn About Story Elements: Character
15 Creative Projects That Help Kids Become Better Readers and Writers

Michelle O'Brien-Palmer

illustrations by
Heidi Stephens

Credits

Cover Design: Jaime Lucero

Student Cover Art: Bean Bag Character: Katelin Davis
Pop-up Dialogue: Carolyn Carr & Natalie Bohner
Character Trait Box: Kathy Chapin & Emily Steyer

Content Editors: Martha Ivy, teacher, Redmond, WA
Martha Ivy's 4th-grade students, Christa McAuliffe Elementary
Nancy Johnston, teacher, Woodinville, WA
Nancy Johnston's 6th-grade students, Wilder Elementary
Valerie Marshall, teacher, Redmond, WA
Valerie Marshall's 4th-grade students, Christa McAuliffe Elementary
Pam Schild, teacher, Woodinville, WA
Pam Schild's 6th-grade students, Wilder Elementary
Nancie Schonhard, teacher, Woodinville, WA
Nancie Schonhard's 6th-grade students, Wilder Elementary
Joyce Standing, teacher, Redmond, WA
Joyce Standing's students, The Overlake School

Other Contributors: Stephanie Garcia, 6th-grade student, Wilder Elementary
Ann Lyman, teacher, Westhill Elementary
Julee Neupert, teacher, Ben Rush Elementary
Eileen Shaner, teacher, Franconia Elementary
Alesha Thomas, 6th-grade student, Wilder Elementary

Young Authors: Colby Emerson
Hannah Gibbons
Greg Lundwall
Willie Nelson
Nick Palmer
Jamie Weaver
Steven Yoo
Terry Yoo

ISBN 0-590-10717-8
Copyright © 1998 by Michelle O'Brien-Palmer. All rights reserved.
Text sections originally published as part of I Love to Read copyright © 1995 by Michelle O'Brien-Palmer
Printed in the U.S.A.

Acknowledgments

I would like to thank the following people for their support and contributions in the creation of *Let's Learn About Story Elements: Character*.

I am especially grateful to the 6th-grade editors for your honest feedback, project recommendations and inspiration for this book. In our seven months together, you made significant contributions in molding *Let's Learn About Story Elements: Character* into its final form. I am very proud to have had the opportunity to work through the writing process with you as my editors.

- Thanks to the student editors from Nancy Johnston's class at Wilder Elementary School. Your project ideas and examples were wonderful. I really appreciate your sharing them with the readers of this book.
- Thanks to the student editors from Pam Schild's class at Wilder Elementary School. Your responsible attitude and great ideas really made a difference in this book.
- Thanks to the student editors from Nancie Schonhard's class at Wilder Elementary School. Your suggestions for materials, material lists, and organizing forms will help the readers of this book immensely.

I also extend sincere thanks to those who helped in the production of this book:

To the young authors for their project examples – Kadi Anderson, Eunice Chung, Tierney Creech, Carey DeAngelis, Colby Emerson, Emily Gibbons, Hannah Gibbons, Meghan Gibbons, Lisa Hails, Billy Harris, Jenny Jones, Janet Kim, Kristina Lin, Justin Lobdell, Edward Lobdell, Greg Lundwall, Matt Marcoe, Andy Meade, Willie Neslon, Tara O'Brien, Sean O'Connor, Nick Palmer, Brian Schnierer, Broderick Smith, Sandy Stonesifer, Michael Strong, Terry Yoo, Steven Yoo, Christi Warren, Jamie Weaver, and Jackie White. To Stephanie Garcia and Alesha Thomas for their great project ideas.

To Valerie Marshall and Martha Ivy's students at McAuliffe Elementary – thank you for inviting me into your classroom. I had such fun talking with you and sharing the process of writing this book. I really appreciate the special effort you made to help me problem solve.

To Joyce Standing's students at The Overlake School – you are so enthusiastic and excited about reading and writing it was inspiring to be among you. Thank you for sharing your projects.

To Martha Ivy, Ann Lyman, Nancy Johnston, Valerie Marshall, Julee Neupert, Eileen Shaner, Pam Schild, Nancie Schonhard, and Joyce Standing for sharing your project ideas.

To Heidi Stephens for your wonderfully inspired illustrations.

To my son, Nick Palmer for your hugs, patience, and writing samples, and to my husband, Gid Palmer for your love and support through all of my creative endeavors. To Evelyn Sansky for your wonderful friendship and to Robert and Marcene Christoverson for your love and guidance.

Let's Learn About Story Elements: Character

is **dedicated** to every child involved in this book

Zach Barth
Samson Chiang
T.C. Colleran
Tierney Creech
Reggie Green
Jay Hellenga
Jenny Jones
P.J. Kapsales
Dustin Marshall
Justin Matts
Luke Myers
David Stolowitz
Jackie White

**Nancie Schonhard's
Students**

Michelle Bauer
Eunice Chung
Colby Emerson
Billy Harris
Diane Jenkins
Peter Johnson
Kristina Lin
Matt Marcoe
Mark Mavis
Andy Meade
Darcy Milne
Broderick Smith
Shon Smith
Sandy Stonesifer
Kacie Tomlinson
Evan Tuck
Chrissy Wakeling
Jamie Weaver

**Joyce Standing's
Students**

Taylor Bass
Dana Bentsen
Andrew Blair
Meghan Blume
Bernie Boglioli
Kaitlyn Bolduc
Jamie Boscow
Chris Brown
Carey Cade
Kaitlin Carbrey
Michael Chealander
Annie Chiu
Julie Culleton
Jordan Davidoff
Jennifer Dickens
Stephanie Diers
Matt Farrington
Andrea Geary
Justin Gedney
Meryl Goodwin
Matthew Hecker
Brady Johnson
Jenny Keaton
Matthew Kesl
Shawn Kidd
Michael Kilburg
Megan Kilkelly
Melissa Kowalchuk
Jessee Kubitz
Nick Landi
Brian Leierzapf
Sean Logue
Katharine Mackey
Elise McKinney
Vimombi Nshom
Pat O'Leary
Jeremy Peronto
Casey Peterson
Nick Ramsey
Robert Reimer
Katie Rooney
Ryan Shane
Kelsey Sikma
Stephanie Sinclair
Michael Slaughter
Conor Thurman
Jake Vela
Erin Whittington
Kaitlin Wight

**Valerie Marshall and Martha Ivy's
Students**

Kadi Anderson
Nathan Belt
Melissa Bernard
Cassie Bolin
Carey DeAngelis
Caitlin Endres
Stephanie Garcia
Jessica Gregson
Lisa Hails
Jeff Hill
Janet Kim
Greg Lundwall
Willie Nelson
Sean O'Connor
Krissy Shea
Michael Strong
Craig Swanson
Alesha Thomas
Christi Warren

**Pam Schild and
Nancy Johnston's
Students**

Colby Emerson
Hannah Gibbons
Greg Lundwall
Willie Nelson
Nick Palmer
Jamie Weaver
Steven Yoo
Terry Yoo

Young Authors

Table of Contents

Introduction

for Parents and Teachers

Let's Learn About Story Elements: Character was written to give children (2nd-5th grade) an enticing selection of reading extension projects focused on story characters. Each project was chosen by other kids as one they would especially recommend. This text is part of the Let's Learn About Story Elements series, which includes books on plot and setting.

Although the text speaks to children directly, it will require adult supervision and guidance in most cases. There are projects which require an Exacto™ knife, scissors and sometimes other potentially dangerous appliances. Each chapter includes front pages with a visual representation of the chapter contents. This is to help kids visually identify those experiences which are of interest to them. Whenever extra information might be helpful to parents or teachers it will be found in italics just under the project head. The second chapter (Keeping Track) includes organizing forms for books, projects and materials. You will also find a reference list at the end of this chapter full of excellent resources for bringing literature into your home or classroom. Throughout the text there are forms for you to use in your classroom. Make as many copies of these forms as you need.

Each project idea in this book is meant to be taken as liberally as possible. There is no one right way to do any project. The more variations created, the more exciting the process will be.

Foreword to Kids

I love to read! The kids who helped me write this book love reading too. We decided to create three books which celebrate reading and share some of our favorite reading projects with you. We worked together for seven months in a school library which looks much like the illustration on page 5; we shared project ideas, tested those ideas, and finally came up with our list of favorite projects related to story characters. We hope you enjoy these projects as much as we do.

Chapter 2, Keeping Track, was designed to help you organize your project materials and keep track of the books you read and the projects you complete. You can copy these forms and use them to gather your project supplies.

Some projects will be new to you and some may be similar to projects you've made before. Use your imagination to create your own unique projects.

Have fun celebrating your favorite books!

I Love to Read

Chapter 1

Introduction

This chapter provides a brief introduction to each main chapter. *Let's Learn About Story Elements: Character* was written with the help of over 100 kids. They were part of the writing and editing process. The young authors who share their unedited project examples in the book are listed below:

Colby Emerson	Nick Palmer
Hannah Gibbons	Jamie Weaver
Greg Lundwall	Steven Yoo
Willie Nelson	Terry Yoo

Chapter 2: Keeping Track

This chapter is set up to help readers organize and track their books, projects, and project materials. The Book Train allows younger readers an opportunity to proudly display the books they have read. The Track-a-Project Sheet gives readers instant feedback as to the types of projects they have created. The Checklist of Project Decorating Items and the Character Project Supply Sheet are great tools for setting up an area with materials you'll need to create the projects in this book. You will find a reference list at the back of this chapter which gives excellent resources for extending the reading process.

Chapter 3: Character Projects

The projects in this chapter allow readers to explore story characters more fully. Younger children can start with identifying the characters in the story by making a simple Accordion Book. Creating Sponge Characters or Character Sculptures naturally facilitates readers' retelling a story through the eyes of the characters. The Talking Character, Pop-up Dialogue and Thumbprint Character projects are great introductions to writing dialogue. The Biography Monologue, Meet the Character and Story Flip Book projects give readers an opportunity to do a more in-depth analysis of story characters.

Chapter 4: Project Recipes

This chapter includes recipes for different project materials, such as modeling clay and papier-mâché.

Keeping Track

Chapter 2

To Help You Keep Track

Project Organizers

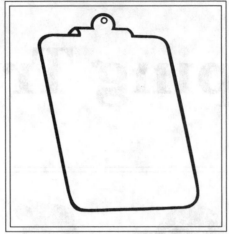

page 15 – page 17

Book Train

page 18 – page 19

Track-a-Project Sheet

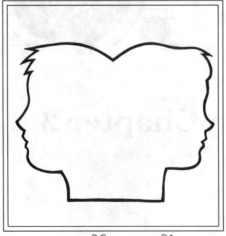

page 20 – page 21

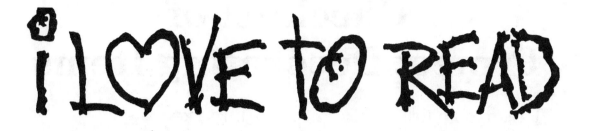

Character Project List

Name:_____

Date: _____

Select one of the following book projects to share with your class:

- ❑ **Sponge Character**
- ❑ **Talking Character**
- ❑ **Character Sculpture**
- ❑ **Bean Bag Character**
- ❑ **Cookie Characters**
- ❑ **Story Flip Book**
- ❑ **Character Accordion Book**
- ❑ **Character Magnets**
- ❑ **Character Trait Box**
- ❑ **Thumbprint Characters**
- ❑ **Pop-Up Dialogue**
- ❑ **Biography Monologue**
- ❑ **Character Mask**
- ❑ **Meet the Characters Book**
- ❑ **Character Story Doors**

Checklist of Project Decorating Items

- ❏ aluminum foil
- ❏ beads
- ❏ beans
- ❏ bottle caps
- ❏ brass fasteners
- ❏ buttons
- ❏ cans
- ❏ cardboard
- ❏ cardboard tubes
- ❏ clay
- ❏ colored moss
- ❏ colored paper
- ❏ colored pencils
- ❏ colored plastic wrap
- ❏ computer paper
- ❏ construction paper
- ❏ cookie cutters
- ❏ cotton balls (colored)
- ❏ cotton swabs
- ❏ crepe paper
- ❏ drinking straws
- ❏ egg cartons
- ❏ fabric paint
- ❏ fabric scraps
- ❏ feathers
- ❏ felt squares
- ❏ film containers
- ❏ finger paints
- ❏ glitter
- ❏ glue stick
- ❏ googly eyes
- ❏ hangers
- ❏ lace
- ❏ magazines
- ❏ margarine tubs

- ❏ markers
- ❏ milk cartons
- ❏ newspapers
- ❏ plain paper
- ❏ paper clips
- ❏ paper cups
- ❏ paper plates
- ❏ paper scraps
- ❏ pastels
- ❏ pie tins
- ❏ pipe cleaners
- ❏ popsicle sticks
- ❏ ribbon
- ❏ sand
- ❏ shells
- ❏ spices
- ❏ sponges
- ❏ spools
- ❏ stickers
- ❏ string
- ❏ tagboard pieces
- ❏ tissue paper
- ❏ toothpicks
- ❏ twigs
- ❏ wallpaper pieces
- ❏ wire
- ❏ wood scraps
- ❏ wrapping paper
- ❏ yarn
- ❏ _____
- ❏ _____
- ❏ _____
- ❏ _____
- ❏ _____
- ❏ _____

Character Project Supplies

My Character Project Supply Sheet

Name:

My Project is:_____

To do my project I will need:

___ Recipe:_____
page #

Writing Tools
___ pencils
___ pens
___ markers
___ crayons

Art Supplies
___ glue
___ scissors
___ felt squares
___ ribbon
___ fabric paint
___ paint brush
___ tempera paint
___ glitter
___ dried beans
___ googly eyes
___ Exacto™ knife
___ ruler
___ other

Paper Supplies
___ form: page #
___ plain paper
___ construction paper
___ craft paper
___ tagboard
___ cardboard
___ cardboard box
___ contact paper
___ colored paper

Other Possible Items
___ book
___ ink pad
___ paper cup
___ tape
___ paper scraps
___ sponge(s)
___ pan
___ balloon
___ butter knife
___ hole punch
___ plastic sewing needle
___ yarn/cord
___ newspaper
___ sand
___ plastic detergent bottle
___ oven
___ costume

Book Train

The book train is a fun way younger readers can proudly display the books they have read.

Materials:
Colored paper
Scissors
Page 19
Pencil/crayons
Laminating materials
Glue

Goal:
To keep track of the books you've read in a train you can display.

Steps:
1. Make a copy of the train form on page 19.
2. Draw yourself in the train engine.
3. Write the book title and the date you finished reading the book inside the train car. Draw your favorite character in the window.
4. Glue the car and engine together.
5. Each time you read another book fill out a train car.
6. Hang the book train in your room.

Book Train

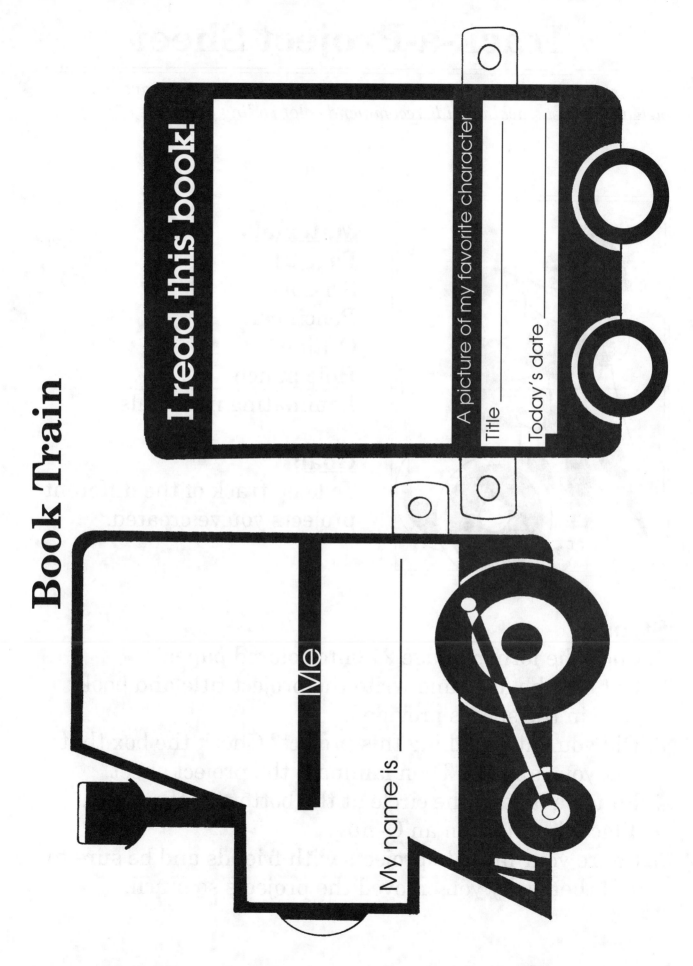

I read this book!

A picture of my favorite character

Title

Today's date

Me

My name is

Track-a-Project Sheet

These sheets help kids monitor and evaluate the projects they have completed. For fast tracking, kids recommend color coding each type of project.

Materials:
Page 21
Scissors
Pencil/pen
O-Ring
Hole punch
Laminating materials

Goal:
To keep track of the different projects you've created.

Steps:
1. Copy the form on page 21 onto colored paper.
2. Cut out the form and write the project title and book title in the spaces provided.
3. Did you enjoy making this project? Check the box that fits your answer. Then laminate the project sheet.
4. Punch a hole in the circle at the bottom of the sheet. Place the sheet on an O-ring.
5. Share your favorite projects with friends and be sure to tell them why you enjoyed the projects so much.

Character Project Sheet

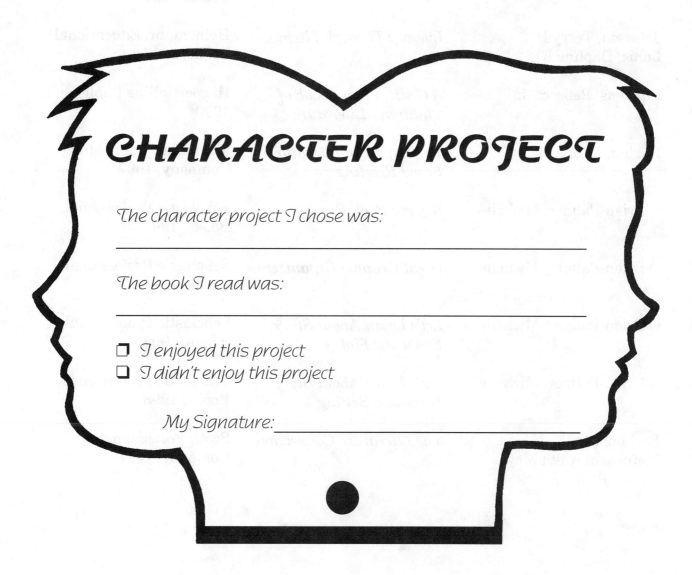

CHARACTER PROJECT

The character project I chose was:

_____

The book I read was:

_____

❏ I enjoyed this project
❏ I didn't enjoy this project

My Signature: _____

Reference Books

Author	Book Title	Publisher
Brown, Hazel Cambourne, Brian	*Read and Retell*	Heinemann Educational Books, 1990
Calkins, Lucy McCormick	*Lessons from a Child*	Heinemann Educational Books, 1986
Johnson, Terry D. Louis, Daphne R.	*Literacy Through Literature*	Heinemann Educational Books, 1987
Luekens, Rebecca J.	*A Critical Handbook of Children's Literature*	HarperCollins Publishers, 1990
Norton, Donna	*The Impact of Literature-Based Reading*	Macmillan Publishing Company, 1992
O'Brien-Palmer, Michelle	*Beyond Book Reports*	Scholastic Professional Books, 1997
O'Brien-Palmer, Michelle	*Great Graphic Organizers*	Scholastic Professional Books, 1997
O'Brien-Palmer, Michelle	*Let's Learn About Story Elements: Plot*	Scholastic Professional Books, 1998
O'Brien-Palmer, Michelle	*Let's Learn About Story Elements: Setting*	Scholastic Professional Books, 1998
Rothlein, Liz Meinbach, Anita Meyer	*The Literature Connection*	Scott, Foresman and Company, 1991

Character Projects

Chapter 3

Chapter Contents

Characters can be like me and you. Or very, very different than we are too.

Authors decide who the characters will be. They create story characters for us to see.

Sponge Character

Talking Character

Character Sculpture

Bean Bag Character

Cookie Characters

Story Flip Book

Chapter Contents

Character Accordion Book

Character Magnets

Character Trait Box

Thumbprint Characters

Pop-Up Dialogue

Biography Monologue

Character Mask

Meet the Characters Book

Character Story Doors

Sponge Character

The Sponge Character can be used in a story dramatization. Younger children really enjoy this project. Adult help may be required with cutting.

Goldilocks and the Three Bears

Materials:
Large soft sponge
Scissors
Pencil and paper cup
Glue
Googly eyes and yarn
Fabric paint

Goal:
To create a sponge character to use in story retellings.

Steps:
1. Select a story character. Using a paper cup, trace a circle on a sponge and cut it out.
2. Draw lines on the sponge (see directions on page 27).
3. Cut partly through the sponge along the top and bottom lines to form finger holes.
4. Cut all the way through the middle line to form a mouth.
5. Make ears, nose, hair and other features out of the rest of the sponge and yarn.
6. Glue the eyes and other pieces to the face.
7. Put your fingers in the finger holes and talk for the character.

Sponge Character Directions

Step 1

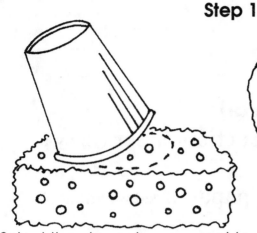

Select the character you want to use. Trace a circle on a sponge using a paper cup.

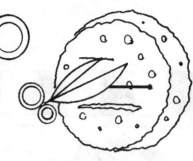

Cut the circle out.

Steps 2 and 3

Draw three lines on the sponge. Cut the top and bottom lines partly through.

Step 4

Cut the middle line all the way through to create a mouth.

Step 5

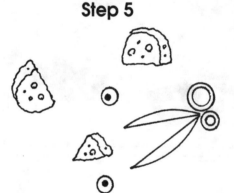

Cut ears, nose, hair, and other items out of the remaining sponge and yarn.

Step 6

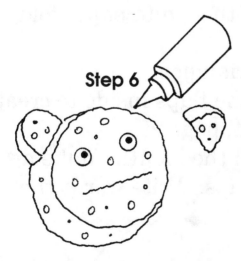

Glue eyes and other features to the face.

Sample

Put your fingers in the finger holes and talk for the character.

27

Talking Character

Creating a Talking Character is so much fun it naturally inspires children to write dialogue.

Materials:
Construction paper (12-by-9 inches)
White paper (81/2-by-7 inches)
Glue
Paper scraps/wallpaper
Scissors
Pencil/pens/markers

Goals:
To start writing dialogue.
To predict what a character might say.

Steps:
1. Fold both pieces of paper in half.
2. Cut a 2-inch line in the center of the white paper fold line (see step 2, page 29).
3. Fold the cut flaps back to form triangles.
4. Open the page and gently push the flaps inside to create the character's mouth (see step 4, page 29).
5. Draw the character's face around the mouth. Make a dialogue bubble out of paper scraps. Write words the character might say inside it.

Talking Character Directions

Step 1

Fold construction paper (12-by-9 inches).
Fold white paper (81/2-by-7 inches).

Step 2

Cut a 2 inch line in the center of the fold of the sheet of white paper.

Step 3

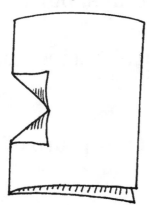

Form two triangle shapes by folding each cut flap back.

Step 4

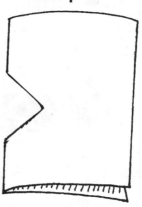

Open up the page and gently push the flaps back inside to form a V-shape.

Step 5

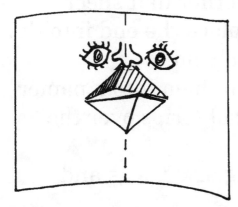

Draw the character's face around the mouth by drawing and pasting features on the page.

Sample

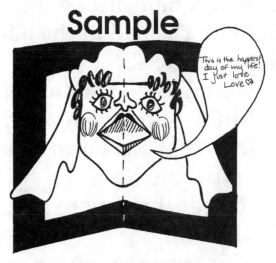

Create a dialogue bubble out of paper scraps.

Character Sculpture

This project is great for all ages and recycles many different materials. Character Sculptures can become the main focus of a story retelling.

Materials:
Plastic detergent bottle
Scissors
Masking tape and glue
Newspapers
Sand (2 cups)
Tempera paint
Material scraps, buttons,
 yarn, etc.
Papier-mâché recipe - page 62

Goal:
To create a sculpture of a story character.

Steps:
1. Remove the cap and pour sand into the bottle.
2 Wad a half sheet of newspaper into a ball.
3. Place the ball in the middle of another half sheet.
4. Twist the sheet around the ball, place the end into the bottle's neck and tape it to form a head.
5. Cut newspaper into strips and dip them into a papier-mâché paste. Form a single layer of strips over the bottle and head.
6. Repeat three more times, creating arms, legs and clothing.
7. Paint your character and add any details.

Character Sculpture Directions

Step 1

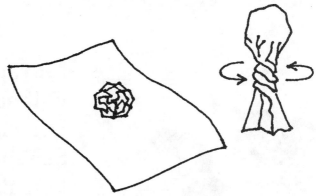

Pour sand into the bottle to keep it stable as you create your character sculpture.

Steps 2 and 3

Tear a piece of newspaper in half. Wad half of the sheet into a ball. Place ball in the middle of the other half and twist around to form a head.

Step 4

Place head into the top of the bottle and tape it.

Step 5

Cut newspaper into strips and dip them into a papier-mâché paste. Form a single layer of strips over bottle and head.

Step 6

Repeat three more times, creating arms, legs or clothing.

Step 7

Paint character and add details with material scraps, etc.

Bean Bag Character

Bean Bag Characters are fun to make and become a story souvenir for years. Adult supervision may be required with younger children for sewing and cutting.

Materials:
Felt squares (2)
Drawing paper
Scissors
Pencil/markers
Glue
Googly eyes
Thread/needle
Dried beans
Yarn
Felt scraps

Goal:
To make a bean bag of your favorite character.

Steps:
1. Draft the character's face on paper.
2. Cut two identical circles out of felt.
3. Cut the nose and mouth out of the remaining pieces of felt.
4. Glue the eyes and facial features to the front circle.
5. Place the front circle on top of back circle.
6. Sew shut all but an inch of the circle.
7. Fill the circle half way with dried beans and sew the opening shut.
8. Glue on yarn or other materials for hair.
9. Share your bean bag with friends and use it to retell a story.

Bean Bag Character Directions

Step 1

Draft the character's face.

Step 2

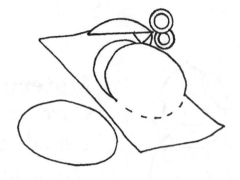

Cut two identical circles out of felt.

Step 3

Cut nose and mouth out of scraps.

Step 4

Glue eyes and facial features on front circle.

Steps 5 and 6

Put front circle on top of back circle. Sew shut all but an inch of the circle.

Step 7

Fill the circle half way with dried beans and sew shut.

Step 8

Glue on yarn or other materials for hair.

Cookie Characters

What could be more fun than creating cookie characters and then eating them? Children of all ages love this project.

Materials:
Cardboard
Pencil/scissors
Oven/pan/butter knife
Gel icing
Sugar cookie recipe - page 61
Scissors
Pastry cloth

Goal:
To bake story character cookies for a book celebration.

Steps:
1. Draw one or more characters on a piece of cardboard. Cut out each character.
2. Make the sugar cookie recipe on page 61.
3. Roll dough on lightly floured pastry cloth.
4. Place the cardboard character on the dough.
5. Use a butter knife to cut around each character. Remove the cardboard.
6. Place each character on a lightly greased baking sheet. Bake at 400 degrees for 10 minutes or until they are light brown.
7. Place cookies on a rack to cool.
8. Decorate each cookie character with icing.

Cookie Character Directions

Step 1

Draw one or more characters
on a piece of cardboard.
Cut out each character.

Step 2

Make sugar cookie
recipe on page 61.

Step 3

Roll dough on lightly
floured pastry cloth.

Steps 4 and 5

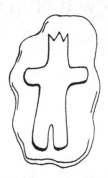

Place cardboard character on top
of the dough and cut around it.
Remove the cardboard.

Step 6

Place cookies on a lightly greased
baking sheet. Bake at 400 degrees
for 10 minutes.

Steps 7 and 8

Cool cookies on a rack. Decorate each character cookie with gel icing or tube
frosting. Eat the cookies during a book celebration.

Story Flip Book

The Story Flip Book is a project idea from Julee Neupert's classroom at Ben Rush Elementary in Redmond, WA. It could easily be adapted to become a plot or setting project.

Materials:
3 pieces of paper
Hole punch
Markers/pencils
Yarn

Goal:
To show how a character grows and changes in a story.

Steps:
1. Fold the three sheets of paper according to the specifications on page 37.
2. Place sheet 1 over sheet 2, sheet 2 over sheet 3, to make 6 pages.
3. Punch two holes at top and tie with yarn. Write the character's name on the top page.
4. Draw a picture of the character early in the story and write a description on page 2.
5. On pages 3, 4 and 5, draw events important to the character. Describe each in a sentence.
6. On page 6, draw a picture of the character at the end of the story and write a description.

Story Flip Book Directions

Steps 1 and 2

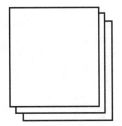

3 inches
1

4 inches
2

5 inches
3

Fold sheet 1 at 3 inches, 2 at 4 inches, and 3 at 5 inches.
Place sheet 1 over 2 , and 2 over 3 to create 6 pages.

Step 3

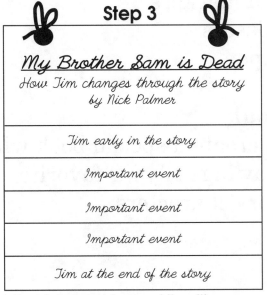

My Brother Sam is Dead
How Tim changes through the story
by Nick Palmer

Tim early in the story

Important event

Important event

Important event

Tim at the end of the story

Punch holes at top and tie with yarn.

Step 4 (page 2)

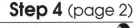

Tim

- Just a kid
- Didn't know about war
- About 10 years old
- Didn't like to do chores

- Played a lot
- Happy
- Free to do what he wanted

Tim early in the story

Important event

Important event

Important event

Tim at the end of the story

Draw the character early in the story and write a description.

Step 5 (pages 3,4,5)

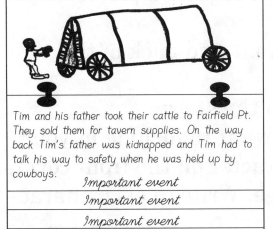

Tim and his father took their cattle to Fairfield Pt. They sold them for tavern supplies. On the way back Tim's father was kidnapped and Tim had to talk his way to safety when he was held up by cowboys.

Important event

Important event

Important event

Tim at the end of the story

Draw and describe an important story event on each page.

Step 6 (page 6)

Tim

- More grown-up
- Hated war
- About 13 years old
- Did all the farm chores

- Had responsibilities
- Sad because his dad, brother and friend died

Tim at the end of the story

Draw the character at the end of the story and write a description.

Character Accordion Book

The character accordion book is a simple and clear way to introduce young children to story characters.

Materials:
Tagboard
Pen/markers
Scissors
Tape

Goal:
To create a special book with drawings of your favorite story characters.

Steps:

1. Trace your page shape onto the tagboard piece.
2. Cut out your book pages.
3. Tape pieces together on the front and back of the tagboard.
4. Think about the characters in the story.
5. Decide which characters you want to include in your book. Draw your favorite character on the front cover.
6. Draw a character on each page. Write in each character's name if you choose.
7. Draw the back cover of your book.
8. Share the book with your friends.

Accordion Book Directions

This project was based on *The Berenstain Bears' New Neighbors*,
by Stan and Jan Berenstain

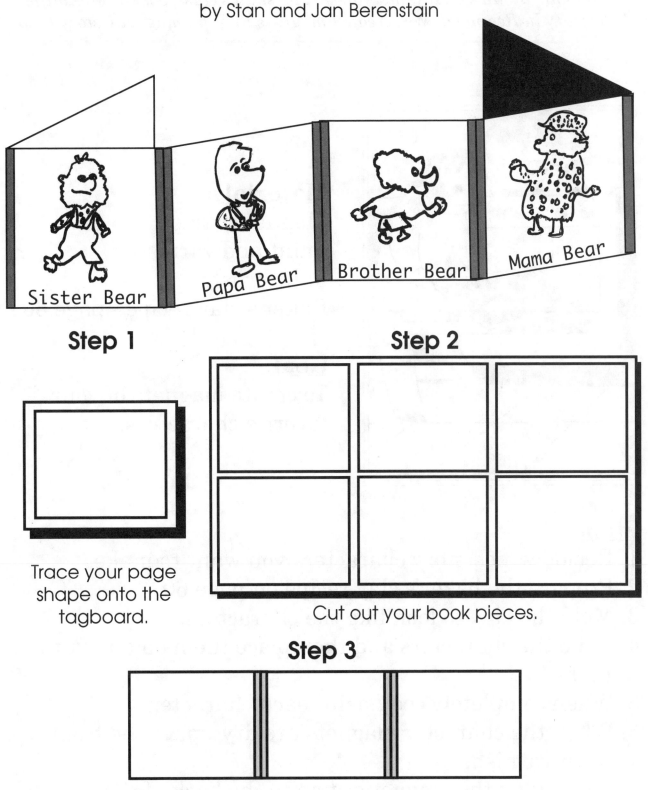

Sister Bear

Papa Bear

Brother Bear

Mama Bear

Step 1

Trace your page
shape onto the
tagboard.

Step 2

Cut out your book pieces.

Step 3

Tape pieces together on the front and
back of the tagboard.

Character accordion book created by Hannah Gibbons

Character Magnets

The students in Martha Ivy and Valerie Marshall's classroom at McAuliffe Elementary in Redmond, WA, created magnets to fit on magnetic story maps.

Materials:
Magnetic strips
Paint and varnish
Paintbrush
Baker's clay recipe - page 60

Goal:
To create magnets of your favorite characters.

Steps:
1. Decide which story characters you want to make.
2. Prepare the baker's clay recipe on page 60.
3. Mold the clay to look like the characters.
4. Bake the characters and then place them on a rack to cool.
5. When completely cool, paint each character.
6. When the character magnets are dry, spray the front with varnish.
7. Later, glue the magnetic strip to the back of the characters.

Character Magnet Examples

Bilbo Baggins and Smaug from *The Hobbit*
created by Nick Palmer

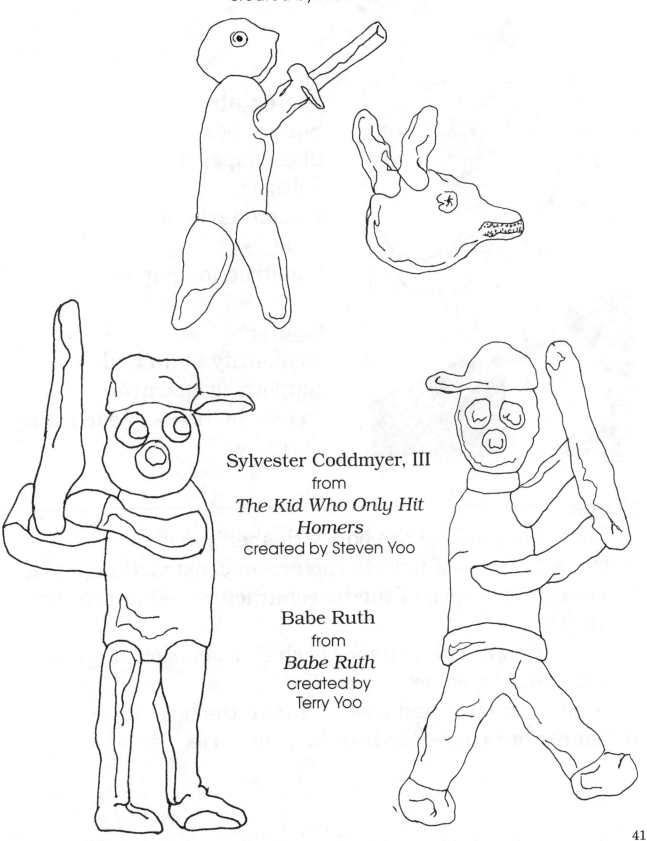

Sylvester Coddmyer, III
from
The Kid Who Only Hit Homers
created by Steven Yoo

Babe Ruth
from
Babe Ruth
created by
Terry Yoo

Character Trait Box

This project was recommended by the students in Joyce Standing's class at The Overlake School in Redmond, WA. They suggest using fabric covered shelf paper to get a more textured look.

Materials:
Square box
Shelf paper (fabric)
Scissors
Pencil/markers
Glue
Construction paper

Goals:
To identify main and supporting characters.
To list the traits of each story character.

Steps:

1. Cover each side of the box with shelf paper.
2. Draw pictures of five characters on construction paper.
3. Think about each of the five characters. What are they like?
4. List a number of traits for each character on strips of construction paper.
5. Glue characters and their traits to the box.
6. Share your character trait box with friends.

Character Trait Box Example

This project was based on *The Mixed-up Files of Mrs. Basil E. Frankweiler*
Character trait box created by Jamie Weaver

Thumbprint Characters

Julee Neupert's students practice writing simple dialogue using their thumb-print characters. The dialogue created can be used later in a reader's theater. A group discussion regarding dialogue is a great way to start this activity.

Materials:
Construction paper (18-by-12 inches)
Pencil and black fine-tip pen
Ink pad (different colored pads are fun)

Goal:
To practice writing dialogue.

Steps:
1. Select two or more story characters.
2. Think of things they might say to each other.
3. Divide the construction paper (18-by-12 inches) into four equal sections.
4. Using an ink pad, make two thumbprints in each of the four sections. Draw arms and legs attached to each thumbprint.
5. Write what you think the characters would say to each other in dialogue bubbles.
6. Share your character conversations with friends.

Thumbprint Characters Example

This project was based on *Charlotte's Web* by E.B. White

Pop-Up Dialogue

The students in Ann Lyman's classroom at Westhill Elementary in Bothell, WA, find writing basic dialogue using this fun pop-up project a truly creative experience.

Materials:
Construction paper:
sheet 1 (17-by-12 inches) and sheet 2 (12-by-9 inches)
Colored/white paper
Glue
Markers/pencils
Scissors

Goals:
To write simple dialogue.
To create a story scene with characters.

Steps:
1. Decide how many pop-ups you want in your project. Fold sheets 1 and 2 in half. Open sheet 2 and draw a story scene on the top quarter of the page.
2. Draw characters for your scene on the white paper and cut them out.
3. Fold sheet 2 with the setting inside. Cut a 2-inch tab from this sheet for each character (see step 3, page 47).
4. Unfold the paper and gently push the cut tabs inside.
5. Center and glue sheet 2 to sheet 1.
6. Once the glue has dried, paste the pop-up characters to the tabs. On the base, write what you think the characters would say.

Pop-Up Dialogue Directions

Step 1

Sheet 1

Sheet 2

(12-by-9 inches)

Fold sheets 1 and 2 in half. Open sheet 2 and draw scene on top quarter of page.

Step 2

Draw and cut out characters.

Step 3

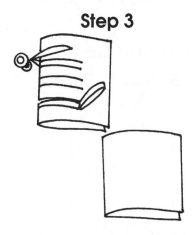

Fold sheet 2 with the scene illustration inside. Cut as many 2-inch tabs as you need for the characters.

Step 4

Open up and gently push cut tabs inside.

Step 5

Center and glue sheet 2 to sheet 1 (don't glue tabs down).

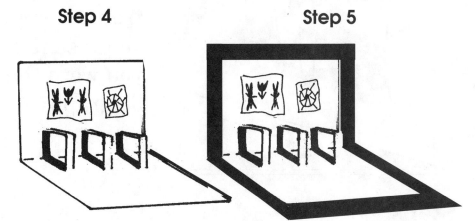

Sample

Step 6

Open up and glue pop-up characters to the tabs. Write dialogue on the base.

Biography Monologue

The students in Nancy Johnston's class at Wilder Elementary in Redmond, WA, thoroughly enjoyed becoming a character from a biography. They dressed up as the character and used their monologue sheets or notecards to give a presentation to the class.

Materials:
Index cards or paper
Costume (you create)
Pencil/markers

Goal:
To present a monologue as if you were the person in the biography.

Steps:

1. Select the person you want to be. Read a biography about this person. Imagine that you are the person.
2. On notecards write:
   - An introduction of yourself (as the character)
   - Something meaningful or significant in your life
   - What your dreams were
   - What your motivation was
   - People important to your personal development
   - Why the biography was written
   - Advice you would give to others
3. Write your notes on paper if you like.
4. Dress up as the character and share the monologue with your friends.

Biography Monologue Examples

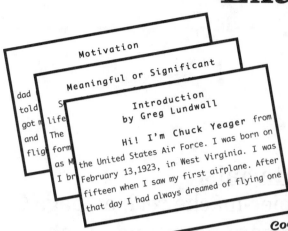

Motivation

dad
told
got ...
and ...
flig...

Meaningful or Significant

S...
life...
The ...
form...
as M...
I br...

Introduction
by Greg Lundwall

Hi! I'm Chuck Yeager from the United States Air Force. I was born on February 13, 1923, in West Virginia. I was fifteen when I saw my first airplane. After that day I had always dreamed of flying one

Cochise
by Willie Nelson

Page 1

I am Cochise, leader of a band of Apache. I was born high in the Dos Cabeza Mountains in eighteen hundred and five. I was taught to hunt at the age of nine by my father. I learned how to survive and live off of the land. As a test, I was left on my own for seven days.

At the age of eleven I was allowed to go on my first hunting trip. I learned to contribute however I could. In time, I became a great hunter capable of leading my people.

My father died and I became Chief at the age of thirty-six. I carried out my father's wish to keep peace with the white for the next twenty three years without conflict.

A mistake by the white eyes led to war. The white eyes thought the Apache had stolen a young whiteboy. I came with several other Apache to see the white eyes, bearing the white flags of peace. We offered to help find the boy who had run away. The white eyes had tricked us and attempted to ambush us. The events that followed are now known as the Cut The Tent Affair. I escaped by slitting the tent and escaping out the back. Many of my relatives were not so lucky. I pledged to avenge their deaths which lead to twenty years of war against the white eyes.

We made peace with the white eyes two years before my death. Only 128 of the 558 Warriors lived to see peace.

I died on June 7th, 1874. I was buried in a sacred Indian burial ground for the Apache chiefs now known as Indian Gorge. I was dressed as a warrior and laid to rest with my horse and dog.

The advice I would share with the youth is that peace and happiness is everything. You take it for granted until it's gone. But what is even more important is to believe in yourself. There are no limits to what you can do.

What motivated me was that because I was the chief, I would have to do the best thing for my people and forget my personal wants. Even if it meant going to war or living on a reservation.

The childhood events and dreams that helped me accomplish all that I did were first, that I wanted to be a great chief and become a great warrior who would be feared by all. I accomplished these things but it wasn't easy.

My life was full of wars, pain, blood and especially tears. In war I had to watch my people die. I lived in pain when my family members were hung.

A biography was written about me because I was an important Apache chief and I was know for terrorizing the white eyes for many years.

The person who helped me most during my life was my father. As an Apache chief he taught me the ways of our people. He also taught me to survive and to preserve the ways of our people.

Character Mask

Julee Neupert's students make character masks. They find masks to be great props for story retellings.

Materials:
Papier-mâché recipe - page 62
Tempera paint and brushes
Scissors
9-inch balloon

Goal:
To create a character mask.

Steps:

1. Blow up a 9-inch balloon to the size of a head.
2. Prepare the papier-mâché recipe on page 62.
3. Tear newspaper into 3 inch strips. Dip the strips into the papier-mâché. Cover only half of the balloon with strips. Repeat three times.
4. Twist the newspaper to make eyebrows, nose and lips. Cover with papier-mâché strips.
5. Add top layer of dry strips creating a smooth surface.
6. Let the mask dry for 7 days. Then pop the balloon and trim the edges.
7. Paint the mask and use it to retell the story.

Character Mask Directions

Step 1

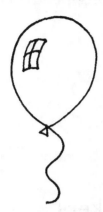

Blow up a 9 inch balloon
to the size of a head.

Steps 2 and 3

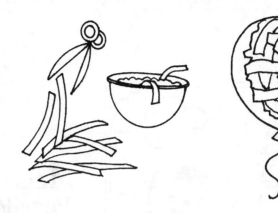

Make the papier-mâché recipe on page 62. Tear
newspaper into 3 inch strips and dip into mixture. Cover
half of the balloon with strips. Repeat three times.

Step 4

Twist newspaper to create
eyebrows, nose and lips.
Cover each with strips.

Step 5

Add top layer of dry strips, creating a smooth surface.
Let the mask dry for 7 days.

Step 6

When completely dry, pop
the balloon and trim the
edges of the mask.

Sample

Paint the mask and use it in a retelling of the story.

Meet the Characters Book

Joyce Standing's students found their Meet the Characters Books provided an opportunity to reveal interesting story information through character descriptions.

Materials:
Pencil/pen/markers
Paper

Goal:
To create a book in which various story characters are introduced.

Steps:
1. Determine the type of book you want to make. You could staple your pages together, or use the accordion book directions on page 39.
2. Select the characters you want to include in your book.
3. Design and create your book cover.
4. Make the title page (see example on page 53).
5. Write about the characters on the left-hand pages and draw the characters on the right.
6. Create a page for comments on which your friends will write what they like about the book.
7. Share your book with friends.

Meet the Characters Book Example

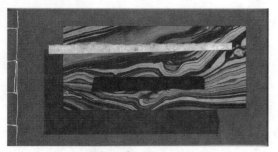

Book Cover

MEET THE CHARACTERS
OF
MOSSFLOWER

Written and Illustrated by
Colby Emerson

Title Page

Martin

When Martin was a young mouse his father, Luke the Warrior, had to go to Salamandastron to fight. He said if he didn't return by fall that Martin should wander off to a differernt land. Martin waited till the end of fall. Luke still hadn't returned. So he set off on his journey.

After awhile he found his way to Mossflower. After wandering around for awhile Martin was captured by the Kotir warriors and taken to the evil queen's dirty cells. ...

name...

Gonff

Gonff was a jolly little mousethief who was happy all the time. One day while he was humming his way through mossflower he was captured. Gonff didn't really care. He knew how to pick locks, so he wouldn't be in any cell for long. Once he fot to the cells, he was thrown in with a young warrior mouse named Martin. When Gonff decided to get himself out of the cell, he got his new friend Martin out too.

After that they went through every battle and adventure together. When Matin had to go to Salman-dast...

Tsarmina

Tsarmina was a wildcat who had an evil mind and desperately wanted to become ruler of Kotir. So she killed her father, the ruler of Kotir, and she became the ruler. She had no mercy and was determined to defeat Mossflower. Day and night she would be thinking of a way to capture the animals of Mossflower. One day she succeeded by capturing two of the bravest mice in all of Mossflower, Martin and Gonff. But they escaped.

One day while she was out in the battlefields a young fox and his group met her and they became a strong team. Bane the Fox had an evil mind, too. Bane

Character Story Doors

Julie Neupert's students really enjoy this project. It is another versatile project in that it can be used for science, setting, plot, etc.

Materials:
Paper
Pencil/pen/markers
Scissors

Goal:
To create a book in which various story characters are introduced.

Steps:
1. Fold a sheet of paper in half lengthwise.
2. Divide the paper into thirds as on page 55. Then create three flaps by cutting the lines halfway up the page.
3. Draw a picture of a story character on each flap.
4. Describe the characters in the section below each flap.
5. Share your Character Story Doors with your classmates.

Character Story Doors Directions

Step 1

Fold a sheet of paper in half lengthwise.

Steps 2 and 3

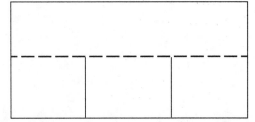

Divide into thirds and cut to the fold to create three flaps.
Draw a picture of a character on each flap.

Step 4

Carrie and her sister and her mom and dad. They are going to their grandpa's house.

Describe the characters in the box below each flap.

Sample
by Justin Lobdell

Share your Character Story Doors with your friends.

Project Recipes

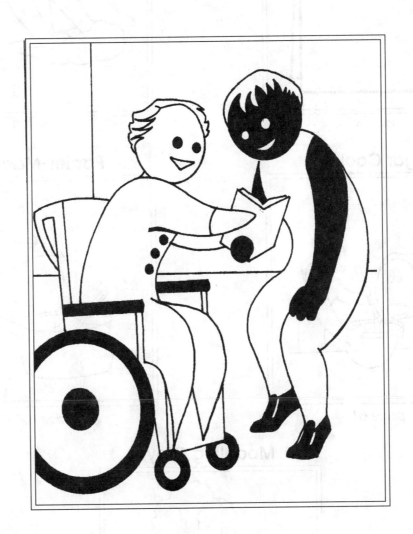

Chapter 4

Chapter Contents

Card Book

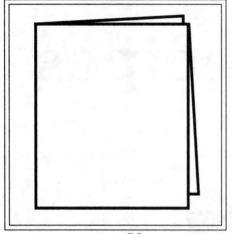

Baker's Clay

Sugar Cookies

Papier-Mâché

Modeling Clay

Card Book

☑ **Materials:**

❑ Sheet of paper   ❑ Pencil   ❑ Markers

Step 1

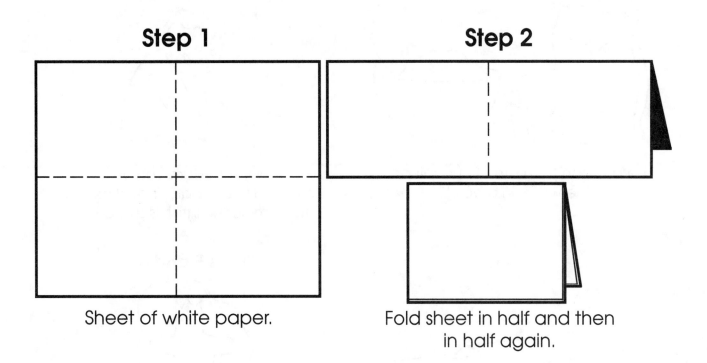

Sheet of white paper.

Step 2

Fold sheet in half and then
in half again.

Step 3

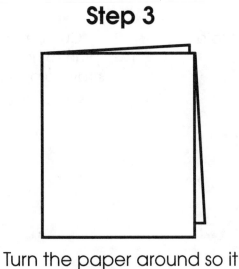

Turn the paper around so it
opens like a card.

Baker's Clay

Adult supervision required.

☑ Materials:

- ❏ Flour (4 cups)
- ❏ Salt (1 cup)
- ❏ Water (11/2 cups)
- ❏ Bowl
- ❏ Spoon
- ❏ Measuring cup
- ❏ Rolling pin
- ❏ Straw
- ❏ Cookie sheet

Step 1

Use a spoon to mix the flour, salt and the water in a bowl.

Steps 2 and 3

Roll the mixture you've created into a ball. Knead for 5 to 10 minutes until it is smooth.

Step 4

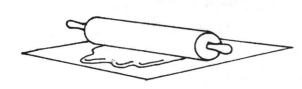

Roll the dough out to a 1/4 inch thickness.

Steps 5 and 6

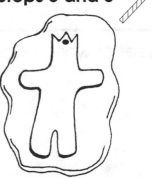

Cut the shapes you want. If you plan to hang the clay objects, use a straw to poke a hole through the top.

Step 7

Bake on a cookie sheet at 250 degrees for 2 hours.

Step 8

Let the shapes dry. Paint them and then spray them with clear varnish.

Let's Learn About Story Elements: Character Scholastic Professional Books

Sugar Cookies

Adult supervision required.

☑ **Materials:**

❑ Powdered Sugar (1 1/2 cups) ❑ Vanilla (1 tsp.) ❑ Baking Soda (1 tsp.)
❑ Butter (1 cup) ❑ Almond Flavor (1/2 tsp.) ❑ Cream of Tartar (1 tsp.)
❑ Egg (1) ❑ Flour (2 1/2 cups) ❑ Hand Mixer/Spoons/2 Bowls

Step 1

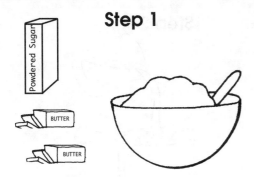

Mix powdered sugar and
butter together until they are
creamy and smooth.

Step 2

Add the egg, vanilla and
almond flavoring to the mixture.
Mix it together well.

Step 3

Mix flour, baking soda and cream of
tartar together in another bowl.

Step 4

Add flour mixture to the sugar and
butter mixture. Blend until it is creamy
and smooth.

Step 5

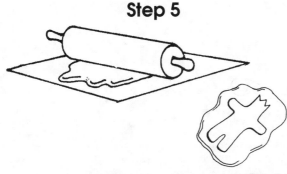

Refrigerate for 2 to 3 hours. Roll
dough 1/4 inch thick on lightly floured
pastry cloth. Cut to desired shape.

Step 6

Place on lightly greased baking sheet
and bake at 375 degrees for 7 to
9 minutes.

Papier-Mâché

☑ Materials:

- ❏ Flour (2 cups)
- ❏ Sugar (1/2 cup)
- ❏ Warm water (1/2 gallon)
- ❏ Cold Water (1/2 quart)
- ❏ Saucepan (1 medium size)
- ❏ Measuring cup (1)
- ❏ Spoon

Step 1

Pour flour and sugar into
the pan and stir.

Step 2

Pour the warm water into
the flour/sugar mixture.

Step 3

Boil the mixture until it is
smooth and clear.

Step 4

Add the cold water to the
mixture to thin it out.

Step 5

Take the pan off the stove.
Use the papier-mâché paste with
projects while it is still warm.

Modeling Clay

Adult supervision required.

☑ Materials:

- ❏ Salt (1/2 cup)
- ❏ Hot Water (1/2 cup)
- ❏ Cornstarch (1/2 cup)
- ❏ Cold Water (1/4 cup)
- ❏ Stove
- ❏ Bowl/Spoons
- ❏ Saucepan (1 medium)
- ❏ Measuring cup (1)

Step 1

Pour salt and hot water in a pan. Heat and stir until it boils.

Step 2

Pour the cornstarch in a bowl. Add cold water and stir.

Step 3

Add the cornstarch mixture to the boiling water. Stir it vigorously.

Step 4

Cook the mixture over low heat, stirring continuously until it is stiff. Then let it cool.

Step 5

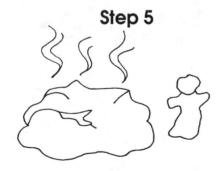

Knead the clay until it's smooth. Create shapes out of it.

Step 6

Let shapes dry 1 to 2 days and paint them.

ABOUT THE AUTHOR
Of...

BOOK-WRITE
BEYOND BOOK REPORTS
GREAT GRAPHIC ORGANIZERS
LET'S LEARN ABOUT STORY ELEMENTS: PLOT
LET'S LEARN ABOUT STORY ELEMENTS: SETTING

Michelle O'Brien-Palmer

Michelle received her undergraduate and graduate degrees from the University of Washington. Her career in educational curriculum development and design spans twenty years.

Michelle works with students and teachers in five to six different classrooms throughout the school year as she writes each of her books. Children and classroom teachers always play an integral role in the creation of her books and music.

- *Educational Workshops and Inservices*
- *School Assemblies and Workshops*
- *Educational Consultation*

MicNik Publications, Inc. • P.O. Box 3041
Kirkland, Washington 98083 • (425) 881-6476